Fish and Visitors
A Getaway Journal

by

US

_____   _____

made the first entry on

_____ , _____ , _____ .

Others made dated and signed entries until

_____   _____

filled the last page on

_____ , _____ , _____ .

When I return to my house I find that visitors have been there and left their cards, either a bunch of flowers or a wreath of evergreen, or a name in pencil on a yellow walnut leaf or a chip.
—*Henry David Thoreau,* Walden

America's most loved forest dweller and renowned journal keeper, Henry David Thoreau, showed the way to "put up" memories more than 100 years ago. He lived at Walden Pond only two of his forty-five years. Because of his journals, he lives there still in our imaginations. Let Thoreau and the others in these pages speak to you and your friends of nature and people, the ridiculous and the sublime. Let them inspire and entertain you, as you fill the blank pages preserving your memories. Unlike jam in a jar, stories in a journal do not have to be consumed to be enjoyed. Stories last forever, becoming more delicious with each telling.

Fish and Visitors

A car, windows down to allow in the smell of piney woods, threads its way up a narrow road following the sun dappled backs of a pair of bicyclists past tangled black spruce swamps, milk-white birches, lofty red and yellow pines, trillium and fire weed. Turning left at a red-on-yellow fire number it enters a clearing and stops.

Visitors have arrived. They tumble out of the car; find the house key hidden in the well, brush the cobwebs off the lock, and open the door. Bracing themselves against the closed-up smell they race to open the windows and throw the drapes aside letting the cheery midday sun fill the cabin. Sunlight bounces off the white letters on the black cast iron fish hanging over the stove. "Fish and visitors smell after three days," the plaque announces. Its inhospitable message once appealed to someone's ironic humor, so it hangs here year after year.

Recognizing the frailty of walnut leaves, and acknowledging that we are all visitors to this special place, we have gone a step beyond Thoreau. We use the *Getaway Journal.* And we invite all our guests to use it to leave a dated entry describing their stay, or sharing a joke, story or drawing. Please feel free to read what others have written, and to add your two bits.

Fish & Visitors

Are we there yet?

Lord, suffer me to catch a
fish so large that even I in
talking of it afterward
shall have no need to lie.
　—Motto over President
　　Hoover's fishing lodge

—On cool nights we sleep like bugs, under rock heavy Hudson Bay blankets.

Even a fish wouldn't get in trouble if it kept its mouth shut.

—*Anonymous*

*Perched on the loftiest throne
in the world, man is still sitting
on his own behind.*
    — *Michel de Montaigne,
        French essayist*

A fishing rod is a stick
with a hook at one end
and a fool at the other.
    — *Samuel Johnson*

*You know the sky will clear
when you see a patch of blue
sky big enough to make a
pair of Dutchman's britches.*
                    —Grandma

The opinions of the husband of
this house are not necessarily
those of the management.
          —Anonymous

If the sun comes out, hold on to your thumbs. It will stay out as long as you don't let go.

     —Grandpa

America's most prolific bird must be the pink plastic flamingo designed by Donald Featherstone in 1957. Two years short of its fortieth birthday, 20 million of its descendants desecrate the landscape.

Kissin don't last; cookin do.
          — Anonymous

—We could have peanut butter and toast—if we had toast—if we had peanut butter. Experts disagree about the origins of peanut butter. Some say it has been around since the 1890s. Everyone agrees that peanut butter reached its full potential with the 1918 invention of the pop-up toaster.

_____

_____

_____

_____

_____

_____

_____

_____

_____

_____

_____

_____

_____

_____

_____

_____

_____

_____

_____

_____

_____

_____

Bear Spotted with Cubs

The life in us is like water in the river. It may rise this year high-er than man has ever known it, and flood the parched uplands; even this may be the eventful year, which will drown out all our muskrats.

—Henry David Thoreau, Walden

A bear is seen eating berries with her cubs near a gravel road. Sunrise reveals that last night's lightning gashed the landmark pine from tip to root, but high winds failed to topple it. Neighbors pick pails of blueberries. The sea yields a fish supper. The golf course yields a hole-in-one. This is cabin news. Spreading through the community like rosy light from a setting sun, it colors the day wonderful.

Bear Spotted with Cubs

To him who in the love of
Nature holds communion
with her visible forms, she
speaks a various language.
    — William Cullen Bryant

Coniferous trees loose great clouds of yellow pollen into the spring forest. Later their more evolved cousins, the deciduous trees, will allow bees to do the work of pollination for them.

When I consider how, after sunset, the stars come out gradually in troops from behind the hills and woods, I confess that I could not have contrived a more curious and inspiring night.
  — Henry David Thoreau

Squirrels, like humans prepare for a "fall shuffle" in August—the month when young born in February and March move out of the parental home to establish independent households.

—Seagull, seagull, sit on the sand. It's never good weather while you are on the land.

— Anonymous

People accustomed to finding vulgarities on the beach may be astounded to find fulgarities in sandy areas. If you find a hollow branch-like tube lying in a sandy spot, it could be petrified lightning formed when a lightning strike fused sand particles into silica. Fulgur is Latin for lightning hence the phenomenon is a fulgarite.

My heart leaps up when I
behold a rainbow in the sky.
— *William Wordsworth*

No one is sure why, but some sandhill cranes paint themselves a bright rust-brown by spreading a mixture of grass and mud on their feathers.

Flowers often grow more
beautifully on dung-hills
than in gardens that look
beautifully kept.
    — St. Francis de Sales

Make spruce gum the way America's indigenous people did. Cut the bark of an evergreen allowing the resinous sap to seep out. When it hardens enough so it will not stick to the teeth, break off a hunk to chew.

The oldest picture book in our
possession is the midnight sky.
— E. Walter Maunder
(1900)

There is pleasure in the pathless woods,
There is rapture on the lonely shore,
There is society where none intrudes,
By the deep sea, and music in its roar...
            — Lord Byron

I Keep Three Chairs in My House

I keep three chairs in my house; one for solitude, two for friend-ship, three for company.

—*Henry David Thoreau,* Walden

one for solitude

The soft click of playing cards against the tabletop amplifies when the game is solitaire. The sound takes up the rhythm of rain drumming on the roof and windows. Flames gutter and surge warming the greystone fireplace as the memory of Grandpa's hands setting its rock warms my heart. I am never alone here. The clouds lift. Stepping outside I recall Thoreau's words, "This is a delicious evening, when the whole body is one sense, and imbibes delight through every pore."

two for friendship

Thoreau spent hours in his canoe playing with a loon. He said it was, "a pretty game played on the smooth surface of the pond, a man against a loon." The object of his game was to place himself nearest where the loon would surface from its deep dive. Checkers and chess place people nearer to one another. Summer girls and local boys playing romantic games carve hearts in the soft wood of the dead log near the road. Sometimes their play turns serious—the cabin hosts a honeymoon pair, their children and their children's children.

three for society

"It's amazing how many great men and women a small house can hold," Thoreau said. Light hearts and clear heads take less room. When the game is hearts, gin or rummy, laughter and good-natured shouts fill the air.

I Keep Three Chairs in My House

This very sun, this very moon, these stars, this very order and revolution of the universe, is the same which your ancestors enjoyed, and which will be the admiration of your posterity.
— Michel de Montaigne

*In play there are two
pleasures for your choosing—
the one is winning; and the
other losing.*

— Lord Byron

Society fatigues me inexpressibly.
So much so, that finding fault
with every one, I have only
reason enough to discover
that the fault is in myself.
        — Mary Wollstonecraft

Eating should be done in silence, lest the windpipe open before the gullet, and life be in danger.
　　　　— The Talmud

Cards were at first for benefits designed, sent to amuse, not to enslave the mind.
          — David Garrick
            (1717-1779)

Books that you may carry to the fire, and hold readily in your hand, are the most useful after all.
          — Samuel Johnson

Peaches are unquestionably a very beautiful and palatable fruit, but the gathering of them for market is not nearly so interesting to the imagination as the gathering of huckleberries for your own use.
   — Henry David Thoreau

*If the Supreme Creator had
meant us to be gloomy, he
would it seems to me, have
clothed the earth in black,
not in that lovely green,
which is the livery of
chearfulness and joy.*
  — *Frances Brooke (1769)*

*If it were the fashion to go
naked, the face would be
hardly observed.*
— Mary Wortley Montagu
(1717)

*The English call checkers,
"draughts." At one time
they called checkers,
"women's chess."*

There are books…which rank in our life with parents and lovers and passionate experiences.
— *Ralph Waldo Emerson*

*I would rather fight with my
hands than my tongue.*
  — Dolley Madison

_____

_____

_____

_____

_____

_____

_____

_____

_____

_____

_____

_____

_____

_____

_____

_____

_____

_____

_____

_____

_____

A child should always say what's true
And speak when he is spoken to,
And behave mannerly at table;
At least as far as he is able.
— Robert Louis Stevenson

To have enough to share—
to know the joy of giving; to
thrill with all the sweets of
life—is living.
— Anonymous

The optimist fell ten floors.
Each time he passed an
onlooker in a window he
shouted, "All right so far."
— *Anonymous*

Home Owner's Labor Day Turkey and Ham Bake

Step 1: Find a safe, legal, and sandy spot for a fire.

Step 2: Dig a hole three feet deep and three to four feet in diameter in the sandy spot.

Step 3: Gather enough rocks (larger than a grapefruit, but smaller than a basketball) to line the bottom and sides of the hole.

Step 4: Gather enough hardwood to keep a hot fire burning on top of the rocks for three hours. Lay the wood on top of the rocks filling the hole. Pile kindling on top of the wood. Light the fire.

Meanwhile prepare a ham and turkey of equal size (up to 15 pounds) for roasting in the pit. Trim fat if desired and wrap the ham and turkey separately in a double layer of foil. Wrap each foil bundle securely in an old blanket. Tie each bundle tightly with wire making a carrying handle with a loop. Soak each bundle thoroughly in water.

When the fire burns down leaving only hot rocks in the hole rake the coals away, drop the turkey (breast side down) and ham in the hole. Fill the hole with sand allowing only the wire handles to protrude. After six to six and one-half hours lift the bundles out and serve. Be careful of the hot rocks.

Copyright © 1997 Judith Nelson
Published by   Openbook Press
                      Box 461
                      St. Francis, Minnesota 55070
                      612-753-2583
All Rights Reserved
ISBN 0-9657498-0-0
Printed in the United States
Text and Editing by Judith Nelson
Cover art and pen and ink drawings by Chad Nelson.

Paper: Text- 60# Glatfelter (Recycled)
              Cover- 80# Benefit Vellum Cover (Recycled)

Printed by: Bang Printing, Brainerd, MN.